W9-DIE-608

THE OFFICIAL

GODZILLA™

MOVIE FACT BOOK

THE OFFICIAL

GODZILLA™

MOVIE FACT BOOK

Based on the hit movie from TriStar Pictures

Compiled by
Kimberly Weinberger and Dawn Margolis

SCHOLASTIC INC.
New York Toronto London Auckland Sydney

GODZILLA™

If you purchased this book without a cover, you should be aware that this book is stolen property. It was reported as "unsold and destroyed" to the publisher, and neither the author nor the publisher has received any payment for this "stripped book."

No part of this publication may be reproduced in whole or in part, or stored in a retrieval system, or transmitted in any form or by any means, electronic, mechanical, photocopying, recording, or otherwise, without written permission of the publisher. For information regarding permission, write to Scholastic Inc., Attention: Permissions Department, 555 Broadway, New York, NY 10012.

ISBN 0-590-78627-X

© 1998 TriStar Pictures, Inc.
GODZILLA, BABY GODZILLA and the GODZILLA character designs
TM & © 1998 Toho Co., Ltd.
All rights reserved. Published by Scholastic Inc.
SCHOLASTIC and logos are trademarks and/or registered
trademarks of Scholastic Inc.

12 11 10 9 8 7 6 5 4 3 2   8 9/9 0 1 2 3/0

Printed in the U.S.A.
First Scholastic printing, June 1998

GODZILLA:
THE ULTIMATE MONSTER MOVIE

You're in total darkness and all is silent. Then, slowly, you begin to notice a faint *thudding* sound. The ground beneath your feet starts to tremble with each vibration as your heart matches the noise thud for thud. The walls begin to shake and crack as the sound grows louder, faster. Then you hear an unmistakable roar — that eerily familiar, heart-stopping wail that tells you … this is no ordinary monster movie.

Perhaps the most anticipated film of 1998, TriStar Pictures' *Godzilla* is the brainchild of director/producer/writing team Roland Emmerich & Dean Devlin — the same talented duo who brought you the box-office phenomenon, *Independence Day*. This time, Emmerich and Devlin have cowritten a screenplay that unleashes the terrible lizard on the unsuspecting metropolis of Manhattan.

This is *not* your parents' Godzilla.

Beginning off the coast of French Polynesia, *Godzilla* opens with a bang — literally — as nuclear explosions rock the group of peaceful islands. Zoom in on one lone lizard's egg buried in the fallout and you've got the premise of the film. Godzilla is the unfortunate product of human beings' desire to blow each other up.

Thirty years pass (in movie time, this translates to 1/100th of a second), and Godzilla has grown. And grown. And grown some more. Now the lizard has decided it's time to see the world. After chomping on a floating fish factory in the Pacific Ocean, Godzilla heads off to Panama, where he visits — and consequently destroys — a tiny fishing village.

Godzilla's behavior, needless to say, does not go unnoticed. Before you can say "tuna fish," the U.S. military is hot on his trail. Dr. Nick Tatopoulos, a quiet, unassuming scientist, is pulled into the frenzied search because of his expertise on the effects of radiation. Played by actor Matthew Broderick (world's coolest teen in *Ferris Bueller's Day Off* and Jim Carrey's obsession in *The Cable Guy*), Nick is the hero of the film.

Of course, no hero acts alone. Through a series of events too complex to get into here (in other words, see the movie), Nick teams up with an unlikely trio: aspiring news reporter and ex-girlfriend Audrey Timmonds; an intrepid and reckless cameraman, Victor "Animal" Palotti; and a mysterious Frenchman, Phillipe Roache. Played respectively by Maria Pitillo, Hank Azaria, and Jean Reno, this courageous band of heroes faces off against the giant lizard as he takes on Manhattan.

    Will Nick and his team survive? Can the city of New York be saved? The answer to these and many other questions can be found in the pages of this book. So dive right in and become the ultimate Godzilla expert.

    Thanks to the wonders of computer technology, this Godzilla is sleeker, faster, and more thrilling than any of his big-screen predecessors. In fact, he's largely computer-generated, which means the sky was the limit in making him as bad and buff as he wanted to be. Turn the page for the lowdown on the big guy....

FROM TOP TO TALON:
Godzilla's Vital Stats

1. **MOUTH:** Capable of emitting gale force winds that can send vehicles flying through the air like Ping-Pong balls (yet another commuting hazard for New Yorkers to put up with).

2. **TEETH:** Over five feet long, these pearly whites would demand some heavy-duty dental floss. (Helicopter blades can be a real pain to remove.)

3. **ARMS:** Massive and powerful, these bulging biceps are particularly skilled at burrowing through subway tunnels.

4. **TALONS:** Six feet long and able to rip through steel as though it were paper.

5. **LEGS:** Michael Jordan has nothing on this lizard. His vertical leap could clear a New York skyscraper (a big one). And don't let his size fool you—this reptile can travel at speeds of up to 300 mph!

6. **TAIL:** A handy appendage if you're looking to wipe out an entire city block in one swoop. This particular one is 256 feet long, which means it leaves a room about 10 minutes after he does.

WHO'S ON THE MENU?
Your Guide to the Cast

DR. NIKO TATOPOULOS   FILE #001X

AKA:	Nick or the "Worm Guy"
Occupation:	Biologist
Employer:	U.S. government, Nuclear Regulatory Commission
Hair color:	Brown
Eye color:	Brown
Height:	5' 10"
Marital status:	Single*

Survivor or lizard food?: Survivor (Duh. He's the hero.) Nick's the only one who figured out what Godzilla is, and what he's done.

*Nick is still pining for ex-girlfriend Audrey Timmonds (see file #002X). Even carries around pictures of Audrey—a slightly pathetic yet somehow endearing quality.

AUDREY TIMMONDS   FILE #002X

```
AKA:            No known aliases
Occupation:     Assistant to
                Charles Caiman*
Employer:       WIDF-TV
Hair color:     Blond
Eye color:      Blue
Height:         5' 7"
Marital status: Single
```

Survivor or lizard food?: Survivor

*Audrey aspires to be a news reporter but
her attempts at success are foiled time
and again by her boss (see file #006X).

VICTOR PALOTTI   FILE #003X

```
AKA:            Animal
Occupation:     Cameraman
Employer:       WIDF-TV
Hair color:     Dark brown
Eye color:      Brown
Height:         5' 11"
Marital status: Married*
```

Survivor or lizard food?: Survivor**

*Victor is married to Lucy Palotti
(see file #005X).

**In a slight break with tradition,
this second male lead manages to avoid
the inevitable "buddy" death scene. A
refreshing moment in movie history.

PHILLIPE ROACHE   FILE #004X

AKA: No known aliases
Occupation: Secret Service agent;
                anonymous insurance
                agent; anonymous
                cab driver*
Employer: French government
Hair color: Dark brown, flecked
                w/gray
Eye color: Brown
Height: 6' 1"
Marital status: Unknown**

Survivor or lizard food?: Survivor

*Phillipe is the foreign man of
mystery and a master of
impersonation. His only complaint:
can't find a decent cup of French
roast coffee.

**Foreign men of mystery are generally
single, but one never knows.

LUCY PALOTTI   FILE #005X

AKA: No known aliases
Occupation: Unspecified TV station
                  employee and best
                  girlfriend to Audrey
                  Timmonds
Employer: WIDF-TV
Hair color: Brown
Eye color: Hazel
Height: 5' 6"
Marital status: Married*

Survivor or lizard food?: Survivor**

*Lucy is married to Victor Palotti
(see file #003X).

**Perhaps the most intelligent of the
group, Lucy spends most of the film
safely in her apartment, watching the
action on TV.

Charles Caiman
the name you
trust in news

CHARLES CAIMAN   FILE #006X

AKA: "Gutter Slime," "Puke
                  Chunks"*
Occupation: News anchorman
Employer: WIDF-TV
Hair color: Dark brown
                  (what's left of it)
Eye color: Brown
Height: Short**
Marital status: Married

Survivor or lizard food?: Survivor

*Courtesy of Lucy Palotti

**Actual height could not be confirmed,
but under 5'5" is probably a safe bet.

THIS IS JEOPARDY!

Well, not exactly. There are no cash prizes to win. But go ahead, try your luck anyway. And find out how much you really know about *Godzilla*. Remember: You must phrase your response in the form of a question. Answers are on page 63 but no peeking till you're done.

1. Nick's research suggests that exposure to radiation has caused these creatures to grow beyond their normal size.

2. In his search for clues to the origin of the mutant lizard, Nick visited these two foreign countries before arriving in the U.S.

3. This New York mayor feared the destruction of Manhattan would hinder his approval ratings during an election month.

4. Godzilla eventually meets his end on this famous New York landmark.

5. Biologist Nick is an employee of this government agency.

6. This Japanese word for Godzilla is based on a sailor's song about a sea dragon.

7. Nick's worm study takes place near this infamous nuclear power plant.

8. Undercover agent Phillipe Roache masquerades as these two types of workers.

9. This aide to Mayor Ebert warns him to watch his weight and stop eating candy.

GO FIGURE:
A By-the-Numbers Survey

Year of nuclear explosion
that created Godzilla: 1968

Number of years Nick
studied earthworms at
Chernobyl: 3 years

Percentage Nick's worms
increased in size due to
radiation: 17%

Number of times Nick's
last name is mispronounced: 4 times

Number of times Nick is
referred to as the "Worm Guy":   5 times

Number of Tatopouloses
listed with Manhattan's
directory assistance: 0

Length of Godzilla's foot: 45 feet

Number of years Mayor
Ebert has held office: 4 years

Number of Hershey Kisses Mayor Ebert eats in a day:	**64 candies**
Number of years Nick and Audrey dated:	**4 years**
Number of years since Nick and Audrey broke up:	**8 years**
Percentage of buildings in New York that Phillipe claims to represent as an insurance agent:	**13%**
Pounds of fish used to lure Godzilla to Flatiron Square:	**20,000 pounds**
Cost per pound of the fish:	**$2.59**
Total cost of catering:	**$51,800**
Number of people who could fulfill their Recommended Daily Allowance of protein by eating this fish:	**14,396 people**
Number of dump trucks needed to haul the fish to Flatiron Square:	**12 trucks**
Number of cans of air freshener it will take to get rid of the fish smell:	**1,362 cans**

Number of nuclear submarines that go after Godzilla:	3 subs
Number of eggs initially spotted by Nick and Phillipe in Madison Square Garden:	3 eggs
Number of eggs actually in Madison Square Garden:	228 eggs
Number of tunnels that lead off the island of Manhattan:	5 tunnels
Number of people told to evacuate Manhattan when Godzilla arrives:	3,000,000
Number of these people who will need psychotherapy as a result of Godzilla's visit:	1,289,520*

*The rest were already in psychotherapy as a result of simply living in New York.

Dear Diary

ATTENTION: STOP READING!

This is the point in our story where you pass this book over to a friend. If you don't have any friends, pass it to a family member (and try to get out more). Then, have this person ask you to supply parts of speech (noun, adjective, etc.) listed within the following diary entries.

Unless you have a really great memory, write your answers down and then plug them into the appropriate places. The results will give you a rare glimpse into the deepest feelings of the characters in the film.

No peeking!

Dear Diary,

_____! What am I going to do? I've done a ter-
exclamation

rible thing. I feel _____. I ran into Nick today
adjective (emotion)

while he was _____ at the drugstore. He was
"-ing" verb

so _____ to me. He even took me back to his
adjective

_____ and told me about his _____.
place   *noun*

But then I saw the tape. The label read: _____.
movie title

I couldn't help myself! I _____ it. Now Nick
verb (past tense)

has lost his _____. And it's all my fault! I've
noun

got to think of a way to _____ him.
verb

> More later,
> Audrey

P.S. Caiman is such a _____!
noun (farm animal)

Dear Diary,

I can't _____ it! Audrey really _____
    verb   verb (past tense)
my feelings. Now I have no _____ and I'm
                              noun
stuck here in _____. Not to mention that
               place
Godzilla is _____ and may have already laid
            adjective
his _____. I have to find those _____
    noun (plural)   noun (plural)
before it's too late. It's the only way to _____
                                            verb
New York.

I knew I should have stayed in _____.
                                  place
I wonder how my _____ are doing?
                animal (plural)

Till tomorrow,

Nick

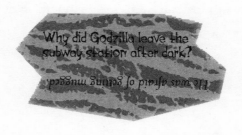

Why did Godzilla leave the
subway station after dark?

He was afraid of getting mugged.

28

Dear Diary,

Oh, how I hate _____. The _____
                        place   adjective
streets, the _____ people, and, worst of all, the
                  adjective
_____. Is there no one who can make a
    noun
_____ cup of _____? If only I were
    adjective   noun (drink)
back in _____. There, they know how to
            place
_____ a _____ meal.
    verb   adjective
        How can I _____ this Godzilla? If my
                          verb
_____ hadn't been so _____, this
    noun   adjective
_____ would never have been _____
    noun   verb (past tense)
in the first place. I cannot _____ my country.
                                    verb

                        Phillipe

P.S. What would Elvis _____ at a time like this?
                              verb

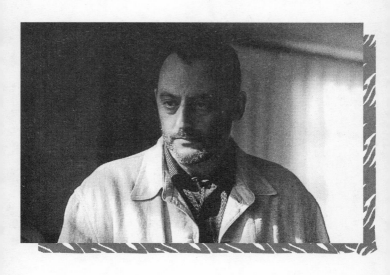

How many Baby Godzillas can you
fit in an empty subway station?

None. If you filled it with Baby Godzillas, it
wouldn't be empty.

WEAPONRY:
How to Bring Down a Mutant Lizard

A look at the tanks, helicopters, and assorted missiles used to *try* and take down Godzilla.

Confidential and extremely scientific measurements can be found on the "Nuisance to Godzilla Scale," or NGS for short. The scale ranges from 1 (about as annoying as a pesky mosquito) to 10 (causes some serious lizard damage).

AIM-9 Sidewinder Air-to-Air Missile

Length:	9' 5"
Weight:	190 lbs.
Maximum speed:	Supersonic (faster than the speed of sound)
Targeting system:	Active infrared (heat-seeking)
NGS:	5*

*Would have been a lot higher had Godzilla been a warm-blooded creature.

M1A2 Abrams Main Battle Tank

Weight: 63 tons

Maximum speed: 42 mph

Crew: 4 (commander, driver, gunner, and loader)

Armament: 120mm smooth-bore cannon

NGS: 4*

* Given its maximum speed, this thing would be lucky to catch a cold, much less a leaping lizard.

Apache AH-64D Attack Helicopter

Height: 3,590 cm

Empty weight: 5,342 kg

Maximum speed: 260 kph

Crew: 2 (pilot and co-pilot/gunner)

Armament: • M-D M230 30mm chain gun
                    (automatic cannon), 625 rounds
                    per minute

                  • Hellfire high-explosive infrared
                    guided missiles

NGS: 1*

* Over the teeth and through the gums, look out stomach—here it comes!

Los Angeles Class Nuclear Attack Submarine (SSN)

Length: 360'

Weight: 6,900 tons displaced

Maximum speed: 20+ knots (23+ mph)

Crew: 13 officers, 116 enlisted men

Armament: • MK-48 self-propelled guided torpe-
                   does:

                   —Length: 14'

                   —Weight: 3,434 lbs.

                   —Range: 5+ miles

                   —Speed: 28+ knots (32+ miles)

                   • 650-lb. high-explosive warhead

NGS: 7*

*The less intelligent viewing audience may have thought this rated a 10, but you weren't fooled, were you?

F/A-18E Hornet Fighter/Bomber

Length:	60.3'
Maximum takeoff weight:	66,000 lbs.
Maximum speed:	Mach 1.8+
Crew:	1
Armament:	• 20mm vulcan cannon
	• AIM 9 sidewinder missiles
	• General purpose bombs
	• AIM 7 sparrow missiles:
	—Length: 12'
	—Weight: 500 lbs.
	—Targeting system: radar
	—Speed: supersonic
NGS	10*

*This bomber is no joke. Its missiles finally dropped the monster on the Brooklyn Bridge. (The fact that he was trapped in the bridge cables and couldn't move didn't hurt, either.)

TRIVIAL QUESTIONS

Following are some detail-oriented questions that you may not get after seeing the movie only once. So, if you score less than 75%, see the movie again. If you're below 50%, see the movie two more times. And, if you score below 25%, see the movie every day for a week (and write on the chalkboard 500 times, "I will pay more attention when watching *Godzilla*"). To see how you scored, check out the answers on page 64.

1. *Which television station employs aspiring reporter Audrey Timmonds?*

   A. WXYZ Channel 37
   B. WIDF Channel 12
   C. WORD Channel 15

2. *Where was Godzilla born?*

    A. Galápagos Islands
    B. Moruroa Atoll Islands, French Polynesia
    C. Gilligan's Island

3. *What is Animal's real name?*

    A. Luciano Pavarotti
    B. Antonio Banderas
    C. Victor Palotti

4. *Which landmark New York building is damaged by a missile blast during an attempt to subdue Godzilla?*

   A. The Empire State Building
   B. Raul's House of Used Hubcaps
   C. The Chrysler Building

5. What kind of candy does Nick use to keep the Baby Godzillas at bay?

   A. Gum balls
   B. Gummy worms
   C. Raisinettes

6. What kind of ship does Godzilla attack first?

   A. A cargo ship carrying fish
   B. A cruise ship carrying caviar
   C. *The Love Boat* carrying Captain Steubing

7. Which of the following was not used to assault Godzilla?

   A. Missiles
   B. Slingshots
   C. Torpedoes

8. Where did Phillipe hide the device that allowed him to monitor the American military's attempts to pursue Godzilla?

    A. On Colonel Hicks' hat
    B. On Sergeant O'Neal's pocket
    C. On Mayor Ebert's suit collar

9. What song was Nick singing as he happily went about collecting his earthworm samples?

    A. "It's Raining, It's Pouring, the Old Man Is Snoring"
    B. "Singin' in the Rain"
    C. "Raindrops Keep Falling on My Head"

10. **Who is the first New Yorker to see Godzilla?**

    A. The mayor, while eating candy
    B. An old man, while fishing in the East River
    C. Donald Trump, while shopping at
       Bloomingdale's

11. **At which subway station was a trap set to snare
    Godzilla?**

    A. 42nd Street Station
    B. 23rd Street Station
    C. Lenny's Gas Station

12. How do Animal and Audrey escape from the locker room at Madison Square Garden?

A. Through the air vent
B. Patrick Ewing rescues them
C. They befriend a Baby Godzilla who shows them the way out

13. What is the name of the insurance company Phillipe claims to represent?

A. Lloyds of London
B. Scams 'R' Us Insurance
C. La Rochelle Insurance

What's the best way to escape from Godzilla?

Alive!

14. **What agency does Phillipe really work for?**

   A. The French Secret Service
   B. The French Foreign Legion
   C. French's Mustard Company

15. **What was the name of the nuclear power plant that Nick was stationed near before being recruited for the Godzilla crisis?**

   A. Chernobyl
   B. Châteaubriand
   C. Champs Elysées

16. **What does the label read on the videotape that Audrey steals from Nick?**

   A. "How to Catch a Mutant Lizard"
   B. "Earthworms II: The Sequel"
   C. "First Sighting"

17. *What singer does Phillipe mimic to fool the military into thinking he's American?*

   A. Elvis Presley
   B. Michael Jackson
   C. Puff Daddy

18. *What code does Phillipe tell Nick to use when calling the U.S. military for help?*

   A. Code Bumblebee
   B. Code Dragonfly
   C. Code Caterpillar

WHO SAID THAT?
Quotable Quotes

What's a great movie without some great lines to quote after you see it? Test your memory and see if you can recall who said what. Check your speaker recall against the answers on page 64.

A. Nick Tatopoulos
B. Phillipe Roache
C. Sergeant O'Neal
D. Audrey Timmonds
E. Charles Caiman
F. Colonel Hicks
G. Mayor Ebert
H. Godzilla

1. "This is America. You can buy anything." _____

2. "We need bigger guns." _____

3. "You're standing in it." _____

4. "That's a lot of fish." _____

5. "Rooaarrrrr!" _____

6. "Listen, this is the time when the big boys go to work, okay, honey?" _____

7. "That's not true. We fed him." _____

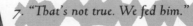

8. "You said this was French roast!" _____

9. "Back off, Gene!" _____

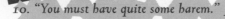

10. "You must have quite some harem." _____

A-MUSING POINTS
To Ponder When There's Nothing Better to Do

If Godzilla roars in the subway, but no one's around to hear him, does he still make a sound?

Don't put off until tomorrow what you can do today because tomorrow you may find yourself dangling from the jaws of a 23-story lizard.

Life is like a box of chocolates. You never know if you're going to get eaten.

Don't walk ahead of me, I may not follow. Don't walk behind me, I may not lead. Walk beside me and you may not get crushed.

If at first you don't succeed, forge a fake press pass, steal your ex-boyfriend's top-secret videotape, and try, try again.

When the going gets tough, the tough go to New Jersey.

It takes a village to raise a child, but who will raise a Baby Godzilla after its mother/father is blown away on the Brooklyn Bridge?

If you give a mutant lizard a fish, he will eat for two seconds. If you teach him how to find a boatload of fish, he'll eat for an hour or so.

The only thing we have to fear is fear itself — plus a 12-ton reptile with an attitude.

The pen is mightier than the sword, but a lizard zapped with radiation can wipe out a skyscraper with one good stomp.

TEST YOUR GODZILLA I.Q.

Yes, it's time once again to find out how big a *Godzilla* fan you really are.

1. **What is the Kobayashi Maru?**

    A. The name of the cannery ship that is attacked by Godzilla in the Pacific Ocean

    B. A test taken by cadets at Star Fleet Academy

    C. Obi-Wan Kenobi's son

2. **Who was the only person to survive the cannery ship attack?**

    A. The captain

    B. The cook

    C. Nobody survived — Godzilla swallowed the ship whole

3. **On what island do we first meet Phillipe Roache and his team?**

    A. Moruroa Atoll Islands

    B. Fantasy Island

    C. Tahiti

4. **Who greets Nick at the sight of the destroyed fishing village in Panama?**

    A. Colonel Alex Hicks

    B. Major Tony Nelson

    C. Godzilla

5. *What does Nick do for a living?*

   A. He's a botanist
   B. He's a physicist
   C. He's a biologist

6. *What does Dr. Elsie Chapman do for a living?*

   A. She's an anthro-
      pologist
   B. She's a paleontologist
   C. She's a psychologist

7. *Whose groceries is Audrey carrying when we first meet her?*

   A. Charles Caiman's, her boss'
   B. Lucy Palotti's, her best friend's
   C. Nick Tatopoulos', her ex-boyfriend's

8. *Where does Audrey first see Nick?*

   A. On a subway
   B. On a television at a diner
   C. On a billboard

9. *What is Mayor Ebert's campaign slogan?*

   A. "Thumbs Up to New York"
   B. "Bigger Is Better"
   C. "I Love New York"

10. *Where does the U.S. military set up its headquarters when Godzilla hits Manhattan?*

   A. Long Island
   B. Staten Island
   C. New Jersey

11. *What brand of doughnuts does Jean-Luc bring to Phillipe?*

   A. Fun-Fun Doughnuts
   B. Tum-Tum Doughnuts
   C. Yum-Yum Doughnuts

12. **What are looters trying to steal when Godzilla crushes their getaway van?**

    A. A pool table
    B. TVs and stereos
    C. A set of golf clubs

13. **What does the military describe as a "negative impact" when it's destroyed?**
    A. The Statue of Liberty
    B. Wall Street
    C. The Chrysler Building

14. **Why can't heat-seeking missiles lock on to Godzilla?**

    A. He's colder than the buildings around him
    B. He's too fast
    C. He can read the minds of the pilots and knows when they're going to fire

15. **Where does Nick ask his cab driver (a.k.a. Phillipe) to take him after losing his job?**

    A. Newark Airport
    B. The Metropolitan Museum of Art
    C. Tiffany's

16. *What does Phillipe's team do to make themselves seem more American?*

    A. They eat apple pie
    B. They chew gum
    C. They wear baseball caps

17. *What body of water does Godzilla dive into after fleeing from the trap in Central Park?*

    A. The East River
    B. The Yangtze River
    C. The Hudson River

18. *How much time do Nick, Audrey, Animal, and Phillipe have to get out of Madison Square Garden once the military is contacted?*

    A. 6 hours
    B. 6 minutes
    C. 6 seconds

19. *What route do Animal and Audrey eventually tell Phillipe to take when fleeing from Godzilla in Manhattan during rush hour?*

   A. The FDR Drive
   B. The West Side Highway
   C. Broadway

20. *What is the number of the cab that Nick gives to Sergeant O'Neal to help him communicate during the final chase scene?*

   A. CAB #MN44
   B. CAB #YZ98
   C. CAB #AB27

21. *Inside what tunnel does the cab become trapped?*

   A. The Lincoln Tunnel
   B. The Holland Tunnel
   C. The Park Avenue Midtown Express Tunnel

22. *What does Nick use to get the cab out of Godzilla's mouth?*

   A. The Jaws of Life
   B. Electric cables
   C. A pair of pliers

Obituary: A Sad Ending for a Misunderstood Reptile

NEW YORK—On the evening of June 1, 1998, the life of the towering lizard known as Godzilla came to an end. After a lengthy and valiant battle involving nearly every weapon known to man, the creature finally succumbed to massive head and body trauma and died on the Brooklyn Bridge.

What can be said about such a lizard? Yes, he was large — larger than any living thing we have ever seen. And, to be sure, the destruction he caused will not soon be forgotten (especially once the repair bills start rolling in).

But, even in the face of this unspeakable terror, let us remember: "Twas beauty killed the beast." No...wait...that's that other monster that caused so much trouble. For Godzilla, the only real crime he committed was being in the wrong place at the wrong time and growing too darn big. He certainly paid a heavy price for his folly.

And so, what lesson can we all take from this horror? Well, it seems there is only one thing left to say: Size does matter.

What's Godzilla's favorite dinner?

Fish and ships

GLOSSARY

Animal: Any of a variety of living things that differ from plants in having cells without cellulose walls. Also, an Italian-American cameraman in his mid-30s.

Apache Helicopter: Military hovercraft capable of firing close-range missiles. Also, a tasty snack for a 23-story lizard.

Chernobyl: Site of the worst nuclear power plant disaster in history. If you don't mind toxic levels of radioactive fallout, it's also a good place to find some cheap real estate.

Code Dragonfly: A top-secret military password that will permit a French Secret Service agent to get patched through to U.S. military intelligence. Of course, now that we've revealed the code word, they'll have to change it.

Dominant Species: What humans currently are; what the one surviving Baby Godzilla may become, depending on how the sequel goes.

Doughnut: A sorry excuse for a croissant. At least, according to Phillipe Roache.

Flatiron Square: Site where the city hoped to trap Godzilla by luring him out with thousands of pounds of fresh fish.

Geiger Counter: Instrument that detects and measures radiation levels in the atmosphere. Incidentally, this device was named after the German physicist who invented it. As if you care.

Gojira: Godzilla's original Japanese name based on a mythological sea dragon that attacked sailors. Isn't it just like Americans to mangle the pronunciation?

Jean-Claude: Member of agent Phillipe Roache's team; indistinguishable from the other member of the team beginning with "Jean-."

Jean-Luc: See "Jean-Claude."

La Rochelle: A fictitious insurance company represented by undercover French agent Phillipe Roache.

Madison Square Garden: Home of the New York Knicks, the New York Rangers, and a brood of very hungry Baby Godzillas.

Moruroa Atoll Islands: Nuclear test site for the French during the summer of 1968. Also, birthplace of Godzilla. If you vacation there, don't drink the water.

Mutated Aberration: Explanation for how a mild-mannered lizard grew into a world-famous monster.

Mutation: A relatively permanent shift in heredity involving either a biochemical or physical genetic change. For example, if a palm-sized lizard egg were exposed to a 14-megaton nuclear blast, the result might be a gargantuan lizard with an insatiable appetite for fish.

Theropoda Allosaurus: An enormous reptile, the likes of which we believe died out in the Cretaceous Period, whose footprints are strikingly similar to a certain mutant lizard we know, but about 10 times smaller.

Worm Guy: Informal way of addressing biologist Dr. Niko Tatopoulos.

Answers from page 18

1. What are Chernobyl earthworms?
2. What are Panama and Jamaica?
3. Who is Mayor Ebert?
4. What is the Brooklyn Bridge?
5. What is the Nuclear Regulatory Commission?
6. What is Gojira?
7. What is Chernobyl?
8. What are an insurance agent and a cab driver?
9. Who is Gene?

Answers to pp. 39–47 Trivial Questions

1.	B	10.	B
2.	B	11.	B
3.	C	12.	A
4.	C	13.	C
5.	A	14.	A
6.	A	15.	A
7.	B	16.	C
8.	C	17.	A
9.	B	18.	B

Answers to pp. 48–49 Who Said That?

1.	B	6.	E
2.	C	7.	A
3.	F	8.	B
4.	A	9.	G
5.	H	10.	D

Answers to pp. 52–57 Test Your Godzilla I.Q.

1.	A*	12.	B
2.	B	13.	C
3.	C	14.	A
4.	A	15.	A
5.	C	16.	B
6.	B	17.	C
7.	A	18.	B
8.	B	19.	C
9.	A	20.	A
10.	C	21.	C
11.	C	22.	B

*Trekkers will note that B is also correct.